BIBLICAL WRITING
SECRETS

Teach Your Teens How to Write Stories That Impact Culture

JUSTICE TILSHER

Copyright © 2024 by Justice Tilsher

All rights reserved.

No portion of this book may be reproduced in any form without written permission from the publisher or author, except as permitted by U.S. copyright law.

Introduction

MY HEART NEARLY LEAPED out of my chest as my younger sisters summoned me. It was a Saturday morning and they were glued to their favorite kids' show. There, in vivid color, were storylines introducing concepts far beyond their years—gay relationships, presented in a manner so casual, it took me a moment to process. In a heartbeat, I reached for the remote and turned off the TV.

"Why did you do that?" They asked me, voices innocent. My insides did a summersault.

It was a moment of awakening, a stark realization that the world of storytelling was no longer a safe harbor but a battlefield of ideologies.

Let's rewind a bit. My journey into the storytelling realm wasn't born out of a desire to enter this battlefield; it started with a love for crafting tales. My passion took off at the tender age of 15 when I ventured into the landscape of writing fan fiction with my friends. I dreamt of crafting a narrative as captivating as Pride and Prejudice or as enchanting as Narnia. I was consumed by stories, living and breathing them, believing in their power to transform lives.

Inspired by a letter to a major film studio from a 13-year-old who claimed stories saved her from the brink of despair, I knew the path I wanted to tread. I yearned to write stories that did more than entertain—they had to resonate, inspire, and perhaps, offer a lifeline to someone in need.

But diving into the world of storytelling was like stepping into a labyrinth of conflicting advice. In every corner of the internet, every author seemed to preach a different gospel of storytelling success. The more I explored, the more bewildered I became. My perfectionist heart sought a clear direction, a universal truth I could anchor my writing to. And it wasn't until I delved into the psychology of storytelling and the word of God, that the pieces began to fall into place.

I uncovered a profound truth: stories are more than a series of events; they are the vessels of truth, designed to resonate with the deepest parts of our being. Since the dawn of time, stories have shaped civilizations, molded moral frameworks, and carried truths from one generation to the next. This was the epiphany that changed everything for me. My mission as a storyteller crystallized—not just to entertain, but to illuminate, to infuse my narratives with the weight of biblical truth and the power to challenge and change minds.

Yet, recognizing my mission was one thing; embarking on it was another. The realization that storytelling had become a contested space, a domain where narratives could shape the future of our culture, was both daunting and amazing. The episode with the kids' show wasn't just a wake-up call; it was a clarion call to action. The stories I had dreamt of writing were no longer a matter of if but a matter of necessity.

The journey to writing my first novel was a marathon of determination and hard work. And when I finally published, achieving the status of a number 1 bestselling author, it was a moment of validation—not for the title, but for the belief that truthful stories could indeed make a ripple in the vast ocean of narratives.

So here I am, a storyteller on a mission, armed with a pen and a conviction as steadfast as ever. In a world where narratives are being manipulated, where the truth is often disregarded in favor of emotion, the call to write stories that spread facts, challenge, and inspire has never been more critical. As I forge ahead, I am reminded of the immense responsibility and the incredible opportunity that lies in storytelling—to cast light into darkness, to guide, to inspire, and to change the world, one truth-filled story at a time.

My Mission

This isn't just writing advice for your teenagers; it's a declaration of war in the battle for our culture's soul. 'Biblical Writing Secrets' is the weapon we're handing to the next generation of storytellers—your teens. It's for those guardians who see the spark of potential in their young writer's eyes and yearn to fan it into a flame that can light up the world with truth and godly wisdom.

We're not just teaching writing; we're spearheading a movement. A movement against the tide of shallow, left-wing entertainment and fleeting trends. This book is a call to arms for parents and teens alike to craft narratives that carry weight, stories that matter, that echo the biblical truths this world is desperately craving.

In the first chapter, we dive into the science of storytelling. Why? Because to change the world, your teen needs to grasp why we're all hardwired for stories. It's not enough to write; they need to understand how to make their words resonate on a fundamental human level, to engage and inspire.

Then, we'll explore God's blueprint for storytelling. This journey is about more than plots and character arcs; it's about aligning with a divine mission. It's about stepping into the calling God has laid out for us storytellers in the world.

Character creation comes next, where the essence of biblical storytelling takes shape. We're not just creating characters; we're sculpting lessons on a page, beings who grapple, struggle, and ultimately embody the journey from darkness to light, from lies to truth.

This book is your guide through this battleground. It's for parents who dream of their teens not only writing stories but writing history. Are you ready to join this crusade? To arm your teen with the power of narrative that can challenge, heal, and transform? Let's rewind storytelling, together.

SECRET #1

Today, we're about to embark on a journey into the heart of storytelling, exploring the crux of why most manuscripts end up decorating the rejection pile and why writer's block is the unwelcome guest in many a writer's room. We're diving deep into the essence of what a story truly is, and let me tell you, it's about to get biblical in the best way possible.

So, you've been there, right? Hammering out a scene that feels as inspired as a Monday morning, only to slam the delete key with the enthusiasm usually reserved for smashing a snooze button. Writer's block doesn't just haunt you; it sets up shop, kicks back, and demands rent for the space it occupies in your brain. And let's not even start on the ominous statistic looming over every writer's dream: the staggering 95% manuscript rejection rate. Makes climbing

Mount Everest in flip-flops seem like a walk in the park, doesn't it?

Here's the kicker: The secret sauce to dodging that rejection slip and breaking free from the shackles of writer's block isn't about crafting the perfect plot twist or engineering a climactic showdown that would make Shakespeare weep. It's about grasping the soul of storytelling. Why? Because if you don't know why your story needs to breathe life into this world, why should anyone else care?

The battlefield of published works is dominated by the elite 3% who finished their journey, with a mere sliver making it onto shelves. The vast graveyard of unfinished dreams and manuscripts isn't a testament to a lack of talent but a missing piece in the storytelling puzzle.

So, what's the difference between you and the literary legends? Between your untold story and the tales that have become the fabric of our culture? The answer lies not in a secret writing elixir but in a roadmap as old as time itself—biblical principles are woven into the very fabric of effective storytelling.

Before we can wield these ancient truths, let's decode the mystery of our brain's affair with stories. Why, in an era where our attention span is outmatched by a goldfish, can a good story rivet us to our seats, eyes glued to the page or screen? There's a magnetic pull to stories, a gravitational force that hooks our brains and whispers, "Forget the dishes, ignore the barking dog; this journey is worth every second."

It's a compelling conundrum, isn't it? We're willing to trade slices of our reality, precious moments of our fleeting lives, to immerse in fictional realms. The power of story transcends the mundane, catapulting us into realms of the unexplored and the yet-to-be-told. It's a testament to the story's unparalleled ability to captivate, to move, and, ultimately, to transform.

James Clear, in "Atomic Habits," touches on the profound truth: humans are wired to seek meaning. Our brains are not just receptors of information; they're meaning-making machines, constantly searching for patterns, lessons, and insights in the chaos of daily life.

This search for meaning is what drives us towards stories. We, as humans, are eternal seekers. Our brains, those marvelous machines, weigh the world around us, sifting through every moment and memory, seeking out significance like a miner panning for gold. Every conversation, every experience, every melody hummed under our breath is a quest for meaning. And, dear writer, it's no different when we delve into a story.

Picture this: You crack open a book, the spine cracking ever so slightly, that fresh ink smell wafting up. Your brain, in its subconscious curiosity, whispers, "Why are we here? What benefit does this tome hold?" Fail to answer, and you'll find your thoughts drifting to lunch plans rather than the unfolding drama. It's not something you articulate, no. You don't quiz your spouse on the existential worth of a

Netflix binge. Why? Because story is encoded in our very DNA. We don't have to ponder it; we feel it.

At its heart, a story is a roadmap, with our brains as seasoned navigators, seeking paths that lead to treasures of insight and understanding. Stories that beckon us forward, promising to enrich our emotional landscape with new perspectives and hard-earned wisdom. When a story ceases to serve this purpose, to feed our minds with significance, our interest wanes, the book closes, the screen darkens.

But what, you might ask, is the treasure we seek on this journey? Here's the revelation: The essence of storytelling is to challenge our beliefs, to question the shadows of doubt and sin that cloud our understanding, and to illuminate our paths with the bright, unyielding light of TRUTH. This is the gold at the end of the narrative rainbow. This is the mission of every tale worth telling.

In its simplest form, a story is about truth. Carve those words into the marrow of your craft.

Because story is about truth, If your narrative doesn't attempt to confront, to question, to offer a beacon of truth, then it is but a shadow of what it could be. A story is not merely entertainment, though joy is a worthy companion on any journey. Story is about igniting that spark within the reader's brain, a spark that whispers, "This matters. This resonates. This is why we must press on."

Research in the field of neurology has shown that when we consume a story that engages us, our brain lights up not only in areas responsible for processing language but also in the parts that we would use if we were experiencing the events of the story ourselves. This phenomenon, known as neural coupling, allows us to empathize with the plot and internalize the story's message on a deeper level.

Moreover, stories that are rich with meaning and moral lessons have been found to increase the release of oxytocin, a hormone associated with empathy and connection. This chemical reaction reinforces the impact of the story, making its message more likely to influence our thoughts and behaviors.

Giving Readers What They Want

Let's get to the heart of the matter: by crafting stories centered around truth, we're giving readers exactly what they crave. This is beyond a narrative strategy; it's fulfilling a psychological need. When truth underpins a story, readers find themselves more than just engaged; they're emotionally and cognitively invested. They're not just passing time; they're on a journey of discovery, learning, and reflection. This is why humans get lost in a "good book" now and then. The feeling of looking at the clock not realizing five hours have gone by. It's not a matter of *wanting* to read, it's a matter of *having* to read. When we are emotionally and psychologically invested in something, we are no longer in control of our actions.

In essence, by weaving truth into the very fabric of our stories, we're not just spinning tales; we're speaking directly to the soul of the reader. This is storytelling at its most powerful and profound. That being said, if you story is not about a core truth, you are going to have a hard time engaging anyone, let alone creating something worth reading.

As we close the curtain on Chapter 1, it's time to take a step back and reflect on the journey we've just embarked on.

Key Takeaways:

- **The Science of Storytelling:** We've uncovered the fascinating interplay between our brains and the stories we encounter. Like a compass pointing north, our minds are drawn to narratives that offer more than just entertainment—they seek meaning, purpose, and truth.

- **The Essence of Meaningful Stories:** Through the lens of timeless tales and the latest research in neurology, we've seen how stories with core truths activate our brains, stirring emotions and fostering empathy. It's these stories that linger, leaving imprints on our hearts and minds.

- **Restoring Storytelling's Soul:** In a world awash with content, the true essence of storytelling often gets lost in the noise. We've explored how stories are not mere distractions but vital tools for survival and understanding, offering insights and guiding lights through the tumultuous journey of life.

- **The Vital Need for Truth in Storytelling:** We dissected the critical role truth plays in a narrative. A story without truth is like a ship without a rudder—aimless and unmooring. We delved into why stories that lack a deeper purpose or fail to challenge our perceptions fall flat, and why manuscripts that don't answer the crucial question of their existence tend to be rejected.

SECRET #2

UNDERSTANDING THAT STORY IS about truth is just part of the equation.

As we dive deeper into the essence of storytelling and its roots in our faith, let's pause and reflect on the profound truth that underpins our entire existence. You see, our journey here isn't by happenstance; it's intricately designed by a Creator who knows us better than we know ourselves. Psalms 139:13-16 says, "For you created my inmost being; you knit me together in my mother's womb". This isn't just poetic language; it's a declaration of our purposeful design by a God who makes no errors, a God who is the epitome of perfection in a world riddled with our daily missteps.

Our pursuit of storytelling, then, isn't just a hobby or a career path; it's a calling. A calling to convey truths, yes, but more importantly, biblical truths. Why? Because at the heart of every moral fiber, at the core of every lesson we've come to hold dear, is a truth that originates from God Himself. Morality, my friends, is not a concept we can claim as our own invention; it's a gift, a guiding light bestowed upon us by divinity.

So why, you might ask, has God chosen this medium—story—to communicate His truths? The answer lies not just in the effectiveness of a narrative to captivate and engage but in its ability to transform. God, in His infinite wisdom, chose storytelling as His vessel to convey the ultimate truth of His existence, His love, and His plan for us.

Consider the vast narrative that is the Old Testament, a testament to God's relentless pursuit of His people, filled with journeys, trials, and revelations. It's a story, real and profound, designed to guide us, to show us the path to righteousness, and ultimately, to Him. And let's not forget the parables of Jesus. God, chose storytelling as His primary method to reveal the Kingdom's truths. These parables weren't casual tales; they were intentional, divine interventions crafted to reach our hearts and minds in a way that direct instruction never could.

The connection between our innate draw to storytelling and God's use of narrative to reveal Himself and His laws is no coincidence. It's a divinely orchestrated strategy, designed to meet us right where we are, in a language we can understand.

Our Responsibilities as Biblical Storytellers

Diving into Psalm 14:89, we uncover a calling that's not just about faith but about action. "As each has received a gift, use it to serve one another, as good stewards of God's varied grace." This isn't merely advice; it's a mission statement. It's about elevating our stewardship beyond simple caretaking to actively enriching the gifts entrusted to us by God, enhancing them for His glory.

Being a steward first requires taking care of the creation. But secondly, we must not only take care of what we have been given temporary custody over, but to also return His creation in a better state than when we found it.

I personally believe that this stewardship calls us to wield our storytelling with purpose. To let this gift sit idly by is to squander a divine opportunity. Our stories have the potential to be vessels of God's word, carrying His truths across the seas of life to harbors of understanding and faith.

When we talk about being stewards of God's creation, it extends far beyond our environmental responsibilities. It's about nurturing the seed of storytelling He planted within us, growing it into a beacon that displays His truth. Our role as biblical storytellers is not a passive one; it's a call to arms, to engage actively in the spiritual battleground of narratives, armed with the light of His word.

As stewards, our first duty is to ensure our narratives are infused with these truths, serving as a mirror reflecting God's teachings. But it goes beyond the message. Our stories must be clean, free from the mire of profanity or blasphemy, aligning with the very essence of God's commandments. Every word, every character's journey, and every plot twist should elevate His teachings, glorifying Him through our craft.

The concept of stewardship in storytelling is a powerful reminder of the impact we can have. It's about realizing the potential within us to inspire, challenge, and bring about change not just in the lives of our readers but in the world at large. The stories we tell today can become the moral compasses for future generations, guiding them through challenges with the light of God's wisdom.

In embracing this role, we take on a mission that goes beyond ourselves, beyond our lifetimes. We become part of a grand narrative authored by God, contributing our verses to His eternal story. It's a profound privilege and a daunting challenge, but in this journey of stewardship, we find our purpose and our path.

Choosing a Truth

If you cannot already tell, I am *very* passionate about this topic! And what follows gets me more excited than drinking a morning cup of coffee with extra creamer (which says a lot!).

At the heart of every story that grips us—whether it's Snow White, The Wizard of Oz, or any tale that has stood the test of time—lies a universal truth.

Now, these sagas might not be rolling out the red carpet for a Sunday school session, but boy, do they hook us in! It's a phenomenon that transcends the bounds of intentional Christian storytelling. They follow a divine blueprint, one that hooks our brains, engages us deeply, and leaves us with impressions that challenge and reshape our beliefs.

It's a startling realization: countless popular narratives are underpinned by biblical truths, often without explicit intention. It's as though the very essence of a compelling story cannot escape the gravitational pull of divine morality. This isn't about preaching or dictating beliefs. Instead, it's about weaving the fabric of truth into our narratives, presenting it in a way that invites the reader to ponder, to question, and ultimately to decide their path. This echoes the core of Christianity itself—God provides His Word, yet it is up to each individual to choose their way, be it in the shadows or His light.

So, as a biblical storyteller, the pivotal question you face is: What belief are you poised to challenge in your readers? It's a question that goes beyond the superficial elements of plot and character. It's about striking the bullseye of your narrative, starting from the very core—starting with *you*.

What is the biblical truth that you feel compelled to share? This initial step is crucial. It's about finding one truth you're passionate about, that you believe can make a difference, and making it the cornerstone of your story. Imagine standing on a global stage, a Christian Eras Tour, your voice reaching every corner of the earth. If there was one thing you could impart, one truth that could change lives, what would it be?

Consider these examples of biblical truths that resonate universally:

- You are loved.

- It's okay to make mistakes.

- Change is inevitable.

- Challenges are growth opportunities.

- Relationships matter.

- Time is precious.

- Failure is part of the journey.

- Always seek forgiveness.

These truths, simple yet profound, are often overlooked or forgotten, yet they are fundamental to our existence and our spiritual journey. They echo the teachings and parables that have been passed down through generations, shaping our understanding of the world and our place within it.

Take inspiration from classic narratives that have conveyed these truths:

- The Prodigal Son teaches us that it's never too late to seek forgiveness.

- The Lion King reminds us that we cannot escape our responsibilities.

- A Christmas Carol shows the transformative power of kindness and empathy.

- Beauty and the Beast reveals that true beauty is found within.

- Around the World in 80 Days encourages us to embrace adventure and personal growth.

This is your moment to stand for what you believe, to share a message that not only entertains but enlightens others. Your story, grounded in biblical truth, has the power to challenge, inspire, and ultimately, change lives.

Choosing a Verse

Now, let's dive into an exercise that's not just fun but foundational. Picture your message, the core truth you've decided to champion, as a verse from the Bible itself. What Scripture embodies the essence of your chosen truth? For instance, if your guiding principle is the belief that "You can do anything you set your mind to," then Philippians 4:13, "I can do all things through Christ who strengthens me," might just be your narrative's cornerstone.

This is your moment to delve into the Scriptures, to find that verse that resonates with the heart of your message. And here's a twist: you might start with a verse and discover the biblical truth that springs from it. Whichever route you take, once you've pinpointed your verse and truth, I urge you to jot them down. Keep this physical reminder close to your writing space, a beacon guiding your storytelling journey.

SECRET #3

Welcome back! Today, we're embarking on an exploration of character creation, the very soul of our stories. Characters, my fellow scribes, are the vessels through which we convey the profound truths that resonate on a deeper level.

Let's dive right in, shall we? Our characters are mirrors reflecting the complexities of human nature, embodying both the flaws and the potential for redemption that we all possess. They are not merely figments of our imagination but echoes of the human condition, intricately designed to embark on a journey toward truth.

At the crux of every memorable story is a character grappling with a fundamental misbelief, a lie that veils their perception of reality. This misbelief, deeply rooted in their experiences, shapes their worldview and sets the stage for their transformational journey. It's their battle with this lie, and the quest for biblical truth, that forms the essence of a compelling narrative. Without this internal struggle, a story loses its purpose, fading into the realm of forgettable tales.

Consider the hallmark of unforgettable narratives - it's not the thrilling sword fights, the daring car chases, or the dramatic family feuds. These are but the shell encasing the motor that propels the story forward: the character's internal struggle with biblical truth. Without this motor, our stories are lifeless, devoid of meaning and impact.

Our readers yearn for characters who are reflections of their flaws, individuals who stumble, and fall, but ultimately rise, guided by the light of truth. It's through these flawed characters that the readers embark on a journey of transformation.

Listen up! This quest for truth is a *battleground*, with Satan wielding lies as his weapon of choice, seeking to lead us astray. Our protagonists, therefore, *must* begin their tale ensnared in a web of deception, clutching onto what we refer to as a *non-biblical truth* that they perceive as reality. Unveiling this lie, and juxtaposing it with the biblical truth, is the task we are called to as biblical storytellers. This non-biblical truth sets the foundation for the character's worldview, and ultimately their transformation. But wait, how on earth do you find a non-biblical truth?

It's simple. A non-biblical truth is simply the opposite of the biblical truth you have already chosen for your story's message. For instance, if you chose the truth, "you should always admit when you make mistakes," the non-biblical lie would be "You should never reveal your mistakes."

This worldview will be what your character spends the entire story fighting against, ultimately leading to the realization of the truth. The journey from believing a lie to discovering the truth is the very point of storytelling. It's about guiding our readers through the narrative, allow-ing them to witness the transformative power of God's truth as experienced by our characters. Our characters, with their flaws, struggles, and eventual redemption, are the driving factor behind a story that "works".

Want VS. Need

At first glance, the concept of "Want VS. Need" seems straightforward. Yet, in the rich tapestry of storytelling, they're threads of gold and iron. The want is a character's conscious desire, a goal shimmering on the horizon, driving them forward. It's the treasure they believe will complete them, the summit of their Mount Everest. Yet, as we, the omniscient narrators know, this is but a mirage, a false summit hiding the true peak beyond.

Our characters are under the spell of a non-biblical belief, a lie that has colored their perception of the world and themselves. This lie dictates their want, driving them towards a goal that, unbeknownst to them, leads away from their true fulfillment.

Consider the wise words from Matthew 7:24-27, where Jesus speaks of building one's house on rock versus sand. Just as the house built on sand cannot withstand the storm, so too are our characters' goals, rooted in falsehood, destined to crumble. Their pursuit of happiness, based on a lie, is as futile as chasing the wind. Why is this? Why can't their goal bring long-term happiness? It's simple: it is based on a LIE! Anything based on a lie, cannot make you happy.

Let's bring this concept to life with examples from characters that have stood the test of time:

- Elizabeth Bennet in "Pride and Prejudice" - Worldview: Her initial *want* is to marry for love, but her *need* is to overcome her prejudices and recognize the true character and worth of those around her, including Mr. Darcy.

- Jean Valjean in "Les Misérables" - Worldview: After years of hardship and injustice, he believes the lie that the world is cruel and unforgiving and that he must look out for himself to survive. His *want*

> is to protect himself and his adopted daughter, Cosette, at all costs, but his *need* is to extend grace and forgiveness to others, reflecting the mercy shown to him by Bishop Myriel.

Without their goals, there would indeed be no story. It's the pursuit of these goals, the climbing of their metaphorical mountains, that keeps us, and our readers, turning the page.

But the journey doesn't end at the summit of their wants. Beyond the mist lies the Promised Land, the place of true fulfillment found in embracing Biblical truth. It's here, at their lowest point, where they must confront the lie that has guided their steps, and open their hearts to the *need*—the truth—that will truly set them free. The need is what will actually make them fulfilled. It's the truth they have been avoiding all this time and can only discover at the end of their journey.

So, let's reflect on these pivotal questions:

- What does my character want at the beginning of the story, and how is this desire a reflection of their non-biblical worldview?

- Why is this goal, this false Promised Land, ultimately incapable of bringing them true happiness?

- And finally, what is their need—the truth that, once embraced, will lead them to genuine fulfillment?

•

Spirit of Fear

2 Timothy 1:7 tells us, "For God has not given us a spirit of fear, but of power and of love and of a sound mind." It's a beacon for us, especially in storytelling, as it highlights the profound battle between fear and truth within our characters. In the realm of storytelling, especially through the lens of biblical truth, this verse serves as a cornerstone.

Our protagonists don't step into the narrative with confidence; they're often ensnared by a spirit of fear, shackled by the very lies their worldview is built upon. This spirit of fear, contrary to the empowerment God offers, distorts their reality, painting their goals with strokes of doubt and hesitation.

Now, let's pivot our gaze towards characters entrenched in classic literature, characters who, like many of us, are wrestling with their fears, fears that keep them from scaling their mountains.

Jean Valjean, from Victor Hugo's "Les Misérables," stands as a testament to this struggle. Valjean, marked by years of unjust imprisonment, steps into the world with a heart heavy with mistrust and fear—fear of society's judgment, fear of returning to a life of bondage. His mountaintop? Redemption and a life of peace. But the specter of his past, coupled with the fear of being unworthy of redemption, hampers his ascent. He's caught in a storm, wrestling with the fear that his efforts for redemption could lead to more suffering for those he loves.

Then, there's Hamlet, Shakespeare's prince of Denmark, ensnared in the web of existential dread and vengeance. His mountain is the pursuit of truth and justice for his father's murder. Yet, a fog of fear envelops him—the fear of the unknown, the fear that his quest for vengeance could lead to his own damnation. This fear paralyzes him, casting long shadows on his path toward resolution.

These characters' journeys are not just narratives; they are mirrors reflecting the duality of our existence—our struggles with fear and the pursuit of a truth greater than ourselves. They remind us that the spirit of fear is not from God but is a barrier to realizing the potential He sees in us. In its basic form, the fear your protagonist feels is always the fear of the biblical truth.

So, as you mold your protagonist, ask yourself:

- What fears keep them from pursuing their goals?
- How does their fear, born from a non-biblical

belief, distort their perception of the truth?

- And when the moment comes, how will these fears shape their journey, either propelling them forward with newfound resolve or ensnaring them in chains of hesitation?

Remember, the essence of their journey is not just in overcoming external trials but in wrestling with and triumphing over the internal tempests of fear, guided by the light of truth. In this struggle, in this dance between fear and truth, lies the heart of a story that speaks to the very core of our being.

SECRET #4

Ah, storytellers, you're back in the writer's nook, where the magic of backstory turns your characters from flat sketches into 3D masterpieces that leap off the page. Today, we're not just dipping our toes; we're diving headfirst into the turbulent waters of our characters' pasts. Buckle up; it's going to be a ride that even the bravest time travelers might second-guess.

Let's crack open the book of life. Every person, your characters included, doesn't start with a clean slate every morning. Nope. We're all walking, talking mosaics of our past experiences. That time you decided against arguing with your dad because, oh boy, the Great Grounding of 2008? Lessons learned, paths altered.

Your characters hold onto their pasts like treasure chests, sometimes filled with more curses than blessings. This treasure, or sometimes, let's admit it, baggage is what we call the "Turning Point." It's that gut-punch moment when their beliefs took a sharp left turn down "This Can't Be Good" Boulevard.

Here's the kicker: The Turning Point is all about unveiling how our beloved characters started romanticizing those non-biblical truths they hold dear. It's that scene where life as they knew it showed them a different, often harsher, reality. But wait! Where exactly does this turning point go? To put it simply, the Turning Point is a scene the author writes to better understand their character's worldview that may or may not go in the actual book. Let me explain.

Example: Lights, Camera, Backstory!

Meet Oliver, the owl with a wisdom rating off the charts, or so he thought. His beliefs are challenged after an academic showdown. Questions flying, Oliver's feathers ruffled, and not in a good way: He fails the test. The outcome? He leaves with the belief in his own intellect, shattered by humiliation. Oliver walks away, his head low, convinced he's not the brightest bulb in the box.

And then there's Cindy, an aspiring ballerina, ready to dance her way into the spotlight, only to have her dreams pirouette right off the stage at the hands of unimpressed judges. The dream she clung to, "I can do anything," morphs into "Maybe dreams are for children."

These aren't just bad days. These are the moments in a character's past that changed who they were for the worst, and display how they believe the lie.

The Moral of the Story?

This is your job as the grand puppeteer when writing the Turning Point scene for your protagonist. Ask yourself: What monumental moment set my character on this path?

How did it warp their worldview by forcing them to turn to a non-biblical belief as truth?

Remember, every character has a past that's prodding them in the back, urging them forward or holding them back. It's your job to shine a light on it – humorously, thoughtfully, and with all the wit you can muster. So grab that pen and let's make those characters as real and as flawed as Aunt Edna's Thanksgiving turkey. Trust me, your readers (and your characters) will thank you for it.

For example, let's turn the pages of classic literature to find a tale that mirrors the emotional depth and transformation we seek in our own characters. Consider Elizabeth Bennet from Jane Austen's "Pride and Prejudice." Elizabeth, vibrant and opinionated, steps into her "Turning Point" scene at Meryton Ball with the expectation of mere social pleasantries. However, her encounter with Mr. Darcy's dismissive remark about her not being "handsome enough to tempt me" serves as her Turning Point. This experience enforces her prejudices against Darcy, embedding the lie within her that pride and societal status dictate true worth, clouding her judgment and guiding her actions throughout much of the tale.

Elizabeth's journey from this Turning Point is a masterclass in character development. It showcases how a single moment can encapsulate a shift in belief.

When crafting your own Turning Point, consider the following:

- What deeply held belief does your character hold as they enter this pivotal scene?

- What specific event or interaction challenges this belief, acting as a catalyst for change?

- How does this event transform their understanding, leading them to embrace a non-biblical truth?

- And most importantly, how does this new belief shape their journey forward, influencing their decisions, actions, and interactions with others?

Remember, the Turning Point is not just a plot device; it's a mirror reflecting the internal struggles and growth of your character. It's a testament to the transformative power of storytelling, where characters are not merely moved by events but are fundamentally changed by them.

The Biblical Mirror

The next scene you are going to write that may or may not go in the book, but will help you better understand your protagonist's worldview is the Biblical Mirror scene.

Picture this: Your protagonist, armed with a shield forged from a non-biblical belief, stands at the edge of introspection yet turns away, blinded by unacknowledged truth. It's not just a missed opportunity; it's a narrative crossroads where destiny is deferred, and redemption waits patiently in the wings.

Consider Ebenezer Scrooge, our miserly friend from Dickens' timeless tale, "A Christmas Carol." He's not just a man with a tight fist and a cold heart; he's a traveler on the cusp of revelation. Each spectral visitor holds up a biblical mirror, beckoning Scrooge to peer into the depths of his soul, to confront the greed and solitude that shackles him. Yet, with each ghostly visitation, Scrooge recoils, choosing the familiar shadows over the daunting light of change.

The Ghost of Christmas Past, in particular, offers a poignant reflection, a window into the moments that molded Scrooge's icy demeanor. Here lies a chance for transformation, a turning point dressed in the garb of yesteryears. But Scrooge, oh dear Scrooge, averts his gaze, tethered still to the earthly treasures that promise warmth but deliver cold.

Crafting the biblical mirror scene in your narrative is akin to setting a stage where your characters are invited to dance with their deepest fears and truths. It's a scene that displays the human capacity for change and resistance.

JUSTICE TILSHER

When etching out this critical scene, paint your protagonist with a palette of stubborn beliefs and fears. Introduce a catalyst, a moment where they have the opportunity to see the truth, but instead turn away, acting on the lie. This is their chance to see beyond the veil of their misconceptions, to grasp the truth that beckons with open arms. Yet, guided by fear, they turn away, embarking deeper into the wilderness of their falsehoods, a decision mirrored in their actions, a testament to their entrapment in the web of deceit they've woven.

This rejection, this deliberate blind spot, is not merely a plot twist; it's the soil from which eventual growth springs forth. It underscores the significance of their impending confrontation with the truth, making their journey toward redemption a narrative of epic proportions, a testament to the power of change and the resilience of the human spirit.

In Cindy's case, this is her having the opportunity to display her dancing skills a second time in hopes of succeeding, but instead of taking the opportunity, she quits dancing, acting on her non-biblical worldview that dreams are a pastime.

The Path Ahead: Crafting the Narrative

By crafting these details about your protagonist in the beginning, you will have a clearer compass when writing the book itself.

In the secrets that follow, we'll dive into the mechanics of plotting, and scene construction, all while keeping your character's spiritual arc at the forefront. But for now, take a moment to reflect on the depth and complexity of the character you've created. They're more than just a figment of your imagination; they're a testament to your commitment to storytelling that doesn't just entertain but transforms.

Prepare yourself for the next phase of our journey together, where your character's path to discovering biblical truth becomes the heart of your story. This is where the real magic happens, where stories become more than tales—they become testimonies of faith, hope, and redemption. Let's continue this journey with the assurance that the truths we weave into our stories have the power to change hearts and minds, fulfilling our noblest purpose as biblical storytellers.

SECRET #5

Here we are, ready to piece together the very essence of what makes a story not just good, but unforgettable. It's about embarking on a journey that doesn't just captivate your readers but transforms them along with your characters. So, let's roll up our sleeves, and maybe, just maybe, find ourselves a little transformed by the end too.

We've talked a lot about internal struggles, worldviews, and the necessity of weaving biblical truths into the very fabric of our narratives. The protagonist's struggle with these truths, their worldview, acts as the engine of our story—without it, we're just revving in place, making a lot of noise but not moving. But an engine without the car is... well, an expensive paperweight. We need to mold the shell, the external conflicts, and dragons (literal or metaphorical), to serve and amplify the internal journey.

Enter the Rewind Storytelling Roadmap. This isn't just a fancy way to say "outline"; it's a blueprint for building stories that resonate deeply because they reflect a journey we're all on: the quest to reconcile our beliefs with truth. Many stories have walked this path before us, leaving breadcrumbs along the way because, let's face it, it works. It takes our flawed heroes from doubt to faith, from confusion to clarity, and in doing so, holds up a mirror to our own journey.

Before we dive deeper, let's get practical for a moment. I want you to have this roadmap in your hands, to scribble on it, to make it your own. So, grab the FREE template at rewind storytelling.com/roadmap, and prepare to journey with me. Each chapter from here on out isn't just a lesson; it's a step. And each step will ask you to plot a point on your story's map.

Now, I hear some of you groaning, "Plotting? I thought this was about inspired storytelling, not pre-calculus." And I get it. The idea of plotting every twist and turn before you write a single chapter can feel a bit... stifling. Like being a Masterchef and being told you can only bake a cake if you follow the recipe to the letter, with no deviations allowed.

But here's the thing: even the best chefs, the Gordon Ramsays of the world, started with a recipe. They learned the rules first—how flavors combine, what happens at different temperatures—before they started throwing ingredients together with the flair of a culinary wizard. The roadmap is your recipe. It's not there to box you in; it's there to ensure that when you do start mixing your ingredients, you're not just hoping for the best. You're working with a tried and true method that leads to success.

You don't have to chart out every detail (unless that's your jam, in which case, go forth and outline with my blessing). But understanding the skeleton of your story, the pivotal moments that drive your character forward, that's non-negotiable. It's the difference between a cake that flops and one that has your readers, I mean eaters, coming back for seconds.

So, as we step forward, keep an open mind. This roadmap, these questions, they're tools in your storytelling arsenal. Use them to build the framework of your narrative. And remember, the beauty of storytelling, much like baking, lies in the freedom to experiment within the confines of the craft. The goal is not just to finish a story (or a cake) but to create something that nourishes delights, and, yes, maybe even changes those who partake in it.

Starting With the End in Mind

As you glance at the Rewind Storytelling Roadmap, you'll notice the 'Promised Land'—not just a destination, but a beacon calling your characters towards their true potential. Yet, akin to Moses and his epic saga, our characters don't merely stroll into their destined glory. Oh no, they're in for a trek through the metaphorical desert, wrestling with doubts and fears, much like we grapple with the idea of fitting another piece of cake into our diet plans.

Our characters, blinded by their falsehoods, view the Promised Land—this bastion of truth—as more daunting than a Monday morning without coffee. Their journey is not merely about reaching a destination; it's about the transformation.

Let's pivot to the concept of 'rock bottom,' a place without hope, where our characters face their darkest hour, not because fate deemed it so, but through their own doing. It's the moment of reckoning, where the weight of their choices comes crashing down, leaving them stranded in the pit they've dug themselves—a pit devoid of latte machines and Wi-Fi.

This pivotal moment, born from the ashes of their decisions, forces them to confront the reality they've shunned—the biblical mirror. Unlike before, when they could afford to ignore its reflection, they now find themselves face-to-face with the truth, with nowhere to hide.

As we march towards crafting this monumental scene, remember, that the road to rock bottom is paved with choices, each bearing its weight of consequences. And just like adding salt instead of sugar to your cake can lead to a baking disaster, the choices your character makes based on lies pave their path to despair.

Yet, within this despair lies the seed of redemption. It's at rock bottom, in their most vulnerable state, that our characters finally glimpse their reflection in the biblical mirror, unfiltered and raw, sparking the transformation that propels them toward the Promised Land.

Crafting the First Chapter

So, gather around as we peer into the looking glass of your protagonist's life before the grand opening of Chapter One. Picture this: your protagonist, armed with a worldview based on a non-biblical truth, stands at the edge of an adventure, peering longingly at a distant mountaintop.

Yet, here they are, rooted to their spot, crippled by a spirit of fear.

But why this paralysis? Ah, the Turning Point, that fateful moment in their past when their beliefs were challenged, leaving them clutching a falsehood as their beacon. This lie, this spirit of fear, has become their worldview, whispering doubts and anchoring them firmly to the ground.

Your opening act's mission, should you choose to accept it, is to highlight these two pivotal elements:

1. The elusive mountaintop

2. And the chains of fear preventing the climb.

Take, for instance, Phileas Fogg from "Around the World in 80 Days." His life, as predictable as the plot of a sitcom rerun, craves the spice of unpredictability. Yet, the rigidity of his routine, his non-biblical truth, shackles him to the ground, preventing him from pursuing the adventures he dreams of. His story begins with a longing gaze at the horizon, yearning for a life beyond his meticulously counted steps.

This leads us to the grand unveiling of the Two Doors—a crossroads of destiny where your protagonist must make a choice. Door #2, bathed in the light of the cross, offers a direct path to redemption and truth: the promised land. Door #1, on the other hand, promises the achievement of the goal through a journey of chaos.

Why, oh why, does your protagonist opt for the path strewn with chaos? Simply put, the fear of confronting their past, the dread of peering into the biblical mirror hanging ominously on Door #2, sends them scampering towards Door #1.

But here's the kicker: regardless of the choice, both doors lead to the Promised Land, to the transformation and truth awaiting them. Yet, encumbered by their flawed worldview, your protagonist views Door #1 as the less daunting option, blind to the circular path it carves back to the very truth they flee.

This pivotal choice, to embark on a journey fraught with self-inflicted trials, in hopes of getting the thing they want, sets the stage for your narrative. It's the spark that ignites the engine of your story, propelling your protagonist into the wilderness in search of their mountain, their dream, all while evading the truth mirrored in Door #2.

Simply put, at the beginning of the story, your character has two choices. See the truth, and abandon their lie by going through door #2, or attempt to get the thing they have always wanted while running from their fear. Of course, they choose door #1. Why? Because they are acting on a lie. They cannot yet see the truth (door #2) because they are acting on a non-biblical worldview and first must go on a journey to learn from their mistakes to see the truth.

So, as your protagonist stands before these two doors in the first chapter, ponder these reflective questions:

- What pivotal event in their past has shaped their current beliefs?

- How does their non-biblical worldview color their perception of their goal?

- Why is the fear of the truth more daunting than the wilderness that lies beyond Door #1?

- How does their decision reflect their inner turmoil and struggle?

Remember, the journey you're about to craft isn't just about reaching a destination. It's about the transformation, the shedding of old beliefs, and the arduous trek through self-doubt and fear. It's about guiding your protagonist, and your readers, through the wilderness to the foot of the cross, where truth and redemption await.

Example of the Two Doors

Let us turn to a chilly Victorian London in "A Christmas Carol," where Scrooge faces his own two-doors moment, courtesy of a ghostly visit from his old partner Jacob Marley. Marley's chains rattle with the warning of a lonely afterlife if Scrooge doesn't change his miserly ways.

Door #2 presents the unvarnished truth of Scrooge's life—that he is a lonely miser who no one cares about, and that people are more important than money.

But ah, Door #1, the path of minimal effort for maximum afterlife comfort. Scrooge, being a pragmatic businessman, sees it as a project management issue—follow the ghosts, tick the boxes, avoid eternal damnation. Simple, right? Yet, his journey teaches him the profound impact of compassion and generosity, a lesson learned not from a checklist but from a heartfelt transformation. Simply put, Scrooge chooses to live a lie, by following the spirits to do the bare minimum it takes to have a peaceful afterlife. He isn't focused on a mindset shift, he is focused on achieving his goal. Which SPOILER ALERT, will not bring him happiness.

So, as you stand at the keyboard, ready to weave your narrative, consider the two doors your protagonist faces. Ask yourself:

- What truth does Door #2 reveal that my character is hesitant to face?

- How does Door #1 appear as the easier, although misguided, path?

- In choosing Door #1, what journey of self-discovery and transformation am I setting my protagonist on?

Remember, the choice at the two doors is just the beginning. The real adventure lies in the journey that follows, a journey that will test their resolve, challenge their beliefs, and ultimately lead them to the truth that sets them free.

SECRET #6

GATHER 'ROUND ONCE MORE, intrepid writers, for the tale of our characters' relentless march towards the metaphorical mountain top, all while Jeremiah 29:11 echoes in the background—a divine voicemail they've stubbornly set to ignore. Ah, the audacity of our heroes, charting a course with the compass of their own making, convinced their map of misconceptions leads to treasure, not a mirage.

Imagine, if you will, our protagonist, burdened with a backpack of lies, trudging up the slope of their own Everest. It's not the snowy peaks of Nepal they face, but a mountain of misconceptions, where the summit promises fulfillment but delivers only the biting chill of realization.

Take, for instance, our hypothetical character, let's call him Johnny No-Mates, who's convinced that relationships are landmines rather than lifelines due to an early loss. Johnny's journey up the mountain is a solo expedition. Each step away from potential bonds is a step deeper into the wilderness of isolation, driven by the fear that opening up might trigger an avalanche of pain. The irony? In avoiding relationships, Johnny's unwittingly hiking towards the very loneliness he dreads, proving that sometimes the greatest risk is playing it too safe.

And let's not forget about Ebenezer Scrooge from "A Christmas Carol," the epitome of ATC (Avoid the Truth at all Costs). Scrooge's approach? Keep humanity at a cold distance, because nothing says "bah humbug" to emotional availability like hoarding wealth and eschewing warmth and kindness. As Scrooge counts his coins, he's blissfully unaware he's accruing a debt of the heart, a deficit no amount of gold can repay.

Or ponder the tale of Elizabeth Bennet and Mr. Darcy in "Pride and Prejudice." Both characters, armed with their prejudices and misjudgments, navigate the social landscape with certainty in their own beliefs. Elizabeth, with her witty defenses, and Darcy, with his aloof demeanor, are on parallel journeys toward the mountaintop of understanding and love, obscured by the fog of their misconceptions. They avoid the biblical mirror of self-reflection and truth, choosing instead the winding path guided by their flawed perceptions.

In all these journeys, our characters are haunted by a ghost—the specter of their turning point, the moment their path diverted onto the road less wise. They don't see the biblical mirror not because it's invisible but because they've chosen blindness over insight, mistaking the echo of their fears for the sound of wisdom.

But fear not, dear scribe, for the plot thickens and the road twists. Our characters' avoidance of the biblical mirror, their detour through the desert of denial, sets the stage for the grand reveal. For it is in the wilderness that the greatest discoveries are made, and it's only by facing their fears that our heroes can find the oasis of truth hidden amidst the sands of deception.

Your guiding questions, as you craft this journey, are:

- How does my character's non-biblical truth blind them to the real promised land, the truth?

- In what ways do they ATC (Avoid the Truth at all Costs)?

- How does this avoidance shape their journey towards the mountaintop, and what falsehoods do they chase?

- How do these choices set the stage for the eventual confrontation with reality, the unavoidable glance in the biblical mirror?

The Bridge

This is it. The moment in the story where our characters confront the most precarious of passages is "the bridge". Ah, this isn't just any old rickety crossing in your story's scenic route. No, this is the point of no return, the Rubicon of our tale, where choices carry the weight of eternity (or at least the weight of a well-crafted narrative).

Our characters, bless their conflicted hearts, have been climbing their metaphorical mountains, dodging villains, and narrowly escaping the consequences of their worldview-governed decisions. They've kept the biblical mirror at a safe distance, using it at most as a coaster for their cup of denial. But here, at the bridge moment, they face a pivotal choice that'll either cement their path or invite them to consider the road less traveled. The bridge moments' job is to present the main character with two choices: turn back and go home, or go up the mountain. Both choices require them to burn the bridge behind them. If they go back down the mountain, they will have to confront their fears, but if they keep going, they have a chance of outrunning the truth in hopes of getting the thing they want.

JUSTICE TILSHER

Imagine, if you will, Elizabeth Bennet at her bridge moment in "Pride and Prejudice." Up to this point, Elizabeth has navigated the social mores of her time with a sharp wit and a firmer grasp of her prejudices. But then comes Mr. Darcy's proposal, as tactful as a bull in a china shop, and Elizabeth's bridge is laid before her. To accept his proposal would mean reevaluating her perceptions of Darcy (and herself), a journey fraught with personal growth but peppered with the risk of heartache. Or, she could retreat, clinging to her initial judgments and beliefs. Of course, she chooses the less painful option by rejecting his proposal.

The bridge moment is a test of character, a fiery crucible that refines our protagonists' mettle. It's where they decide whether to keep trudging toward the deceptive mirage of their mountaintop or to take a leap of faith toward true fulfillment.

So, as you pen this critical juncture, remember: the bridge is where your character's faith in their misconceptions is put to the ultimate test. It's where they choose between the illusion of comfort in falsehood, or the transformative path of truth. It's a decision that shapes not just the chapters that follow but the very essence of your tale.

Your guiding questions, as you chart this course, are:

- What revelation or challenge brings my character to their bridge moment?

- How does this moment illuminate the choice between the safety of their worldview and the perilous path to growth?

- In choosing to cross the bridge by running from the truth, what internal conflicts does my character grapple with, and how do these reflect their deeper fears and desires?

- How does this decision propel them further into their journey, weaving the fabric of their story with threads of consequence and revelation?

SECRET #7

As we delve into the depths of our protagonist's transformational journey, approaching the cliff of what can only be described as rock-bottom. This moment, cloaked in the shadows of despair, mirrors our own spiritual lows, where the absence of light feels most profound, akin to the absence of Christ's comforting presence.

Our protagonist, emboldened by their pursuit of a seemingly noble goal, has been climbing tirelessly. They've weathered the storms of adversity, dodged the arrows of consequence, and, with the summit in sight, they believe triumph is within grasp. This echoes the journey of Jay Gatsby, standing at the edge of his opulent dock, reaching out towards the green light across the bay—a symbol of his unattainable dream.

Yet, as with all pursuits detached from the divine truth, what appears as a pinnacle of achievement is but a mirage, a deceptive edge leading to a precipice. Jane Eyre, on the verge of marrying Mr. Rochester, discovers a truth so harrowing that her envisioned mountaintop crumbles beneath her, revealing the chasm of rock bottom below.

The biblical narrative reminds us of Jeremiah 29:11, a promise of prosperity and hope, yet our characters, in their willful blindness, march to the beat of their own drums, rejecting this divine foresight. This is the moment when they reach the top of the mountain at the climax of the story. They think that they are about to get the very thing they have always wanted.

However, the twist is that this mountain was never a mountain at all. It was a cliff, and your main character just so happens to be standing right on the edge. They stand on the brink, mistaking the edge for a summit, only to be met with the avalanche of consequences—a snowball of their own making, set in motion by their choices, now barreling down with relentless fury.

This is the moment when all of the bad choices the main character has made throughout the story catch up to them and send them tumbling over the edge of the cliff.

This isn't just a fall; it's a plummet into the depths of isolation, a descent into the darkness where the light of truth seems extinguished. It's the chilling moment in "The Great Gatsby" when Gatsby realizes that Daisy's love, the beacon he's been chasing, will never be his—a realization that strips him of all he's fought for, leaving him floating, aimlessly, in his pool, a stark symbol of his rock-bottom.

Similarly, Jane Eyre, upon uncovering the existence of Mr. Rochester's wife, faces her own descent. The revelation shatters her dream of marital bliss, propelling her into a night so devoid of hope, that she flees into the moors, embodying her own journey through the valley of shadow.

This rock-bottom isn't merely a plot device; it's a reflection of life without Christ's guiding light—utterly devoid of hope and filled with despair. It's a moment of profound isolation, where our characters must confront the hollow foundation of their pursuits and the stark reality of their isolation.

The worst part is that they are at rock bottom because they followed a lie. This rock-bottom is their own doing.

As you sculpt this moment into your narrative, ask yourself:

- How does my character's pursuit lead them to this illusion of a mountaintop, only to find themselves on the edge of despair?

- In what ways does their fall to rock bottom mirror their spiritual journey, echoing the absence of divine guidance?

- How can this moment of profound isolation and despair catalyze their eventual redemption and return to the path of truth?

The Truth

Forge ahead, for it is in the depths of rock bottom that the most compelling tales of redemption, resilience, and return to grace are born.

In the shadowed valley of rock bottom, where hope seems but a faint whisper, your character stands, beaten yet unbowed, before a choice that could redefine their very soul. This is the crucible, the moment of utter desolation that paradoxically holds the seed of redemption. Here, they find themselves face to face with the biblical mirror, the truth they've spent a lifetime running from now the only light in the darkness.

This encounter isn't merely about self-realization; it's an awakening, a confrontation with the divine truth that has always been, waiting patiently for the moment of recognition. It's akin to Saul's journey on the road to Damascus, a blinding revelation that what they perceived as truth was but a shadow, and the real truth, the Word of God, has been within reach all along, obscured by their own rebellion and fear.

Jeremiah 29:11 resonates deeply in this moment, a reminder from the Lord of His plans not to harm but to prosper us, to give us hope and a future. Yet, our protagonist, like so many of us, has wandered far from this promise, entangled in the lies of the enemy, believing happiness and fulfillment lie in the pursuits of the world rather than in the embrace of the Father.

At this pivotal crossroads, marked by the presence of two doors once again, the decision before them is stark. Door #1 leads further into the darkness, a continuation of life apart from God, a path of isolation and despair. Door #2, however, stands as an invitation to redemption, to walk in the light of God's truth, embracing the love, forgiveness, and grace He offers. This is the doorway to the cross, to the sacrifice Jesus made, laying down His life that we might find ours in Him.

Choosing Door #2 isn't the path of least resistance. It's a decision to face the pain of the past, confront the lies, and embrace the truth that sets free. It's a commitment to walk through the refining fire, to allow God to transform the ashes of failure into beauty, and to exchange mourning for joy. It requires a death to self, a laying down of the old life to pick up the new life Christ offers—a life marked by His love, guided by His truth, and filled with His purpose.

As your character grapples with this decision, consider the weight of the choice before them:

- How does the revelation of truth in the biblical mirror challenge their long-held beliefs and perceptions?

- What fears and doubts must they overcome to step through Door #2, and embrace the path of redemption?

- How does the concept of grace—a second chance they know they don't deserve—impact their decision?

- In what ways will their choice to accept God's truth and grace mark a turning point in their journey, signaling a break from the past and a step into a new, hope-filled future?

This is the moment your narrative transcends the confines of fiction to touch upon the eternal, the point where story meets testimony, reminding us all of the power of God's redemptive love. Here, in the choice to reject the darkness and step into the light, your character embodies the journey of faith each of us is called to—a journey from death to life, from falsehood to truth, from despair to hope. It's a testament to the transformative power of God's love, a love that meets us even in our darkest hour, offering a way back home.

Here we are, at the precipice of transformation. The journey through valleys of despair and over mountains of false hope has led to this: rock bottom. Yet, even here, in the depth of spiritual and emotional bankruptcy, a glimmer of light breaks through the darkness.

Imagine, for a moment, the profound desolation that envelops your character at rock bottom. It's a place where the shadows of past choices loom large, a dungeon of consequence crafted by their own hands. But amidst the despair, a reflection catches their eye—the biblical mirror, once avoided, is now the only source of illumination in the darkness. This mirror, unlike any other, reflects not just the surface but the soul, revealing the deep scars of sin and the brighter mark of potential redemption.

Consider "The Great Gatsby," where our tragic hero, Gatsby, reaches his rock bottom in the wake of unrequited love and unfulfilled dreams. His pursuit of Daisy, a symbol of his own "mountain top," collapses under the weight of reality and his own illusions. The biblical mirror here might reveal Gatsby's misplaced faith in the material and temporal, urging a turn towards the eternal truths he's neglected.

These characters, each trapped at the nadir of their stories, are confronted with the biblical mirror and the choice it represents. The mirror does not judge; it invites. It offers a glimpse of who they can become if they choose to embrace the truth, to shed the lies that have led them to this desolate place.

And so, your character stands at the threshold of decision. The two doors appear once more, but this time, the choice is informed by the harsh lessons of their journey. Door #1, the path of continued rebellion against God's truth, promises only a deeper descent into despair. Door #2, however, beckons with the promise of redemption, a return to the path God has laid out for them, marked by the cross of Christ.

This choice is deeply personal, yet universally resonant. It echoes the decision each of us faces when confronted with the truth of the Gospel. Do we continue in our ways, or do we surrender to God, accepting His grace and embarking on the path to the promised land?

As your character makes their choice, they embody the essence of spiritual rebirth. The act of choosing Door #2, of stepping towards the cross, is both an acknowledgment of their need for God and a declaration of faith in His power to save and transform. It's a testament to the beauty of grace, the reality that though we fall, we are never beyond the reach of God's loving hand.

Reflect on these questions as you bring your character's journey to its culmination:

- How does the encounter with the biblical mirror at rock bottom challenge and change your character's perception of themselves and their need for God?

- What fears and doubts must they overcome to choose Door #2 and embrace the path of redemption?

- How does their choice reflect the transformative power of God's truth and grace in their life?

- In what ways does your character's journey from rock bottom to redemption mirror the spiritual journey we are all called to embark upon?

This chapter, this moment, is a powerful testament to the grace of God, a reminder that no matter how far we stray, His love remains steadfast, offering us a way back, a path to true fulfillment and peace in Him.

BONUS SECRET (#8)

So, you've ventured deep into the heart of storytelling, sculpted characters that are as real as your quirky neighbor who talks to plants (they're good listeners, apparently), and now you're staring down the 'in-between' scenes. You know, the meat of your story sandwich. This is where the Rewind Storyteller Scene Card swoops in like a superhero with a day planner – it's all about keeping you on track, one scene at a time.

Imagine your scene card as the ultimate guide in your storytelling quest. It's the GPS when you're deep in the narrative woods. The scene card is made up of three boxes:

What Happens

JUSTICE TILSHER

How it Relates to Their Worldview

Character's Decision

Today, we're taking a closer look at our example character, Max, an artist with a vision and a problem as unique as his art.

- **What Happens:** Max is about to have his big break at an art gallery. But there's a catch: he's too nervous to present his work. Instead, his ever-loyal assistant takes the stage. As the assistant basks in the limelight, Max's boss then approaches and demands Max to step up and claim his work. It's showtime, but Max's nowhere near ready for his close-up.

- **How it Relates to Their Worldview:** Here's the thing about Max—he grew up in the shadow of a famous father who was publicly mocked for his profession. Max believes deep down that "People will never see the real you when you are famous". His mountain top, his goal? To gain recognition without ever stepping into the spotlight. This gallery scene is Max's internal battle made external, his crossroads between staying in the shadows or stepping into the light.

- **Character's Decision:** With the pressure mounting and his boss's ultimatum echoing in his ears, Max makes a choice that's as Max as it gets. He grabs a nearby cloth, holding it in front of his face like a shield as he steps onto the stage. It's Max's way of being present without fully exposing himself, a compromise between his desire for recognition and his fear of the spotlight.

And there you have it. Max's scene is a microcosm of his journey—his struggle with identity, recognition, and the role of an artist. Each scene you craft using the Rewind Storyteller Scene Card is a step, a leap, or sometimes a reluctant shuffle toward the ultimate reveal: who your characters truly are when the curtains fall and the lights dim.

JUSTICE TILSHER

This scene card isn't just a tool; it's your narrative compass, guiding you through the tumultuous seas of character development and plot twists. So, whether your character is an artist dodging the spotlight or a superhero grappling with their secret identity, remember: the essence of their journey lies in the choices they make, scene by scene, card by card.

Let's dial in a bit more. You see, each scene card you fill out is a step closer to understanding your character's journey inside and out. It's like being a detective in your own story, piecing together the clues of your character's heart and mind.

For instance, let's say you're writing the scene about Elizabeth Bennet turning down Darcy's marriage proposal because it doesn't align with her ideals of love.

- **What Happens:** Mr. Darcy proposes to Elizabeth despite their odds with one another.

- **How it Relates to Their Worldview:** Up until this point, Elizabeth has spent the story believing that Darcy is a prideful moron who thinks her family a disgrace to society.

- **Character's Decision:** She chooses to remain true to her worldview by rejecting his proposal because her beliefs won't let her do otherwise.

So, as you plot each scene, ask yourself:

- What external event is rocking my character's world?

- How does this event challenge their deeply held beliefs?

- And, most importantly, what decision will they make that propels them forward on their journey to transformation?

By meticulously crafting each scene with these questions in mind, you're not just filling in the blanks—you're weaving a tapestry of moments that collectively tell a story of growth, challenge, and eventual triumph. And remember, every great story is a journey of a thousand steps, or in this case, a thousand scene cards, each one a stepping stone towards that grand, transformative arc.

So grab your scene cards, fellow scribes, and let's embark on this narrative adventure, socks and sandals at the ready. After all, if our characters can face their fears and grow, so can we – one heart-rending scene at a time.

CLOSING

AND JUST LIKE THAT, we've arrived at the end of this book. To all the parents and teen writers out there, you've ventured through the valleys of character development, scaled the mountains of plot twists, and navigated the rivers of narrative tension. You've seen firsthand how a single story can illuminate the darkest corners, challenge the status quo, and offer hope where it's needed most.

Here's the thing: the world is brimming with stories, each waiting for a brave soul to tell it. And that soul, my friends, is you. Yes, you—the one wondering if your story is "good enough," "interesting enough," or "important enough." Spoiler alert: it is. Your story holds the power to inspire change, foster empathy, and spark imagination in ways you can't even imagine.

Parents, your role in this narrative adventure is invaluable. You're not just bystanders; you're the mentors, the guides, the cheerleaders. Your encouragement is the wind beneath your teen writers' wings, propelling them forward when doubt creeps in and celebrating their victories, big and small.

Teen writers, remember: every word you write is a step towards creating the change you wish to see in the world. Your stories are more than just tales; they're reflections of your values, dreams, and the world you envision. So, wield your pen like the mighty sword it is and carve your path through the literary landscape.

Remember, the only story that can't make a difference is the one that's never told.

So, brave storytellers, the world is your canvas, and your words are the brush. Paint a picture that's uniquely yours, and may your stories echo through the halls of time, inspiring generations to come with truth and God's love.

And, if ever you find yourself staring at a blank page, daunted by the journey ahead, just whisper to yourself, "I am a storyteller, and my story matters." Because it does. Now, go out there and make your mark on the world—one word, one story, one masterpiece at a time.

If you are interested in taking your teen's writing journey to the next level, head to rewindstorytelling.com

Made in the USA
Middletown, DE
08 May 2024